On the Wings of Angels

On the Wings of Angels

COMPILED BY GAIL HARVEY

PORTLAND HOUSE

NEW YORK · AVENEL

This 1998 edition is published by Portland House,
a division of Random House Value Publishing, Inc.,
201 East 50th Street, New York, New York 10022

Designed by Liz Trovato

Printed and bound in the United States of Amercia

ISBN 0-517-20369-3

8 7 6 5 4 3 2 1

Introduction

*A*ngels—the very word conjures up an image
of lovely heavenly beings, light and free, the ethereal embodiments of good-
ness and generosity, representations of our hopes. Angels, we believe, are
strong when we are weak and are able to help us when we cannot help
ourselves.

The word "angel" comes from the Greek *angelos,* meaning messenger.
The concept of angels has its origins in the ancient religion of Meso-
potamia. Convinced that there was more to reality than was obvious, the
Mesopotamians believed that the divine power that created the world
communicated with its inhabitants through spirit messengers, angels, who
journeyed on a pathway between heaven and earth.

Angels appear in classical myth and philosophy, in the vision of Shamans,
in Hinduism, Buddhism, Taoism, Zoroastrianism, and Islam, as well as in

Judaism and Christianity. In all traditions, angels serve as messengers of God and are said to hover between heaven and earth. According to many traditions each person on earth has a guardian angel. Indeed, Psalm 91:11 says: "For He shall give his angels charge over you in all thy ways."

On the Wings of Angels celebrates the wonder of God's marvelous messengers. Emanuel Swedenborg writes of his own experience of angels. Robert Burton claims that "Every man hath a good and a bad angel attending on him in particular, all his life long." There are excerpts from the Old and New Testaments, as well as the Koran, and poetic tributes from such well-known writers as Emily Dickinson, James Russell Lowell, Alfred Tennyson, Edgar Allan Poe, and Robert Browning. Included, too, is a touching story by Hans Christian Anderson.

This beautiful book, with its Florentine decorations and evocative drawings and paintings by many artists, including Florence Harrison and Eleanor Fortesque Brickdale, will surely enrich your life with the spirit and the imminence of angels.

GAIL HARVEY

New York
1993

Angels are spirits, but it is not because they are spirits that they are angels. They become angels when they are sent. For the name *angel* refers to their office, not their nature. You ask the name of this nature, it is *spirit*; you ask its office, it is that of an angel, which is a messenger.

SAINT AUGUSTINE

I am well aware that many will say that no one can possibly speak with spirits and angels so long as he is living in the body; many say it is all fancy, others that I recount such things to win credence, while others will make other kinds of objection. But I am deterred by none of these: for I have seen, I have heard, I have felt.

EMANUEL SWEDENBORG

*T*he soul at its highest is found like God,
but an angel gives a closer idea of Him.
That is all an angel is: an idea of God.

MEISTER ECKHART

How shall we tell an angel
　　From another guest?
How, from the common worldly herd,
　　One of the blest?

Hint of suppressed halo,
　　Rustle of hidden wings,
Wafture of heavenly frankincense,
　　Which is these things?

The old Sphinx smiles so subtly:
　　"I give no golden rule,
Yet I would warn thee, World: treat well
　　Whom thou call'st fool."

GERTRUDE HALL

Be not forgetful
to entertain strangers,
for thereby some have entertained
angels unawares.

HEBREWS 13:2

So great is the power of angels in the spiritual world that, if I should make known all that I have witnessed in regard to it, it would exceed belief.

EMANUEL SWEDENBORG

he angels sing the praise of their
Lord and ask forgiveness for those on earth.

THE KORAN

*I*t is not because angels are holier than men or devils that makes them angels, but because *they do not expect holiness from one another, but from God alone.*

WILLIAM BLAKE

But all God's angels come to us disguised:
Sorrow and sickness, poverty and death,
One after other lift their frowning masks,
And we behold the Seraph's face beneath,
All radiant with the glory and the calm
Of having looked upon the front of God.

JAMES RUSSELL LOWELL

Sweet souls around us watch us still,
Press nearer to our side;
Into our thoughts, into our prayers,
With gentle helpings glide.

HARRIET BEECHER STOWE

When one that hold communion

with the skies

Has fill'd his urn where these

pure waters rise,

And once more mingles with

us meaner things,

'Tis e'en as if an angel shook

his wings.

WILLIAM COWPER

*Every man hath
a good and a bad angel
attending on him in particular,
all his life long.*

ROBERT BURTON

The Ministry of Angels

And is there care in Heaven? And is there love
    In heavenly spirits to these creatures base,
That may compassion of their evils move?
    There is: — else much more wretched were the case
    Of men than beasts: but O! th'exceeding grace
Of highest God, that loves his creatures so,
    And all his works with mercy doth embrace,
That blessed angels he sends to and fro,
To serve to wicked man, to serve his foe!

How oft do they their silver bowers leave
    To come to succor us that succor want!
How oft do they .with golden pinions cleave
    The flitting skies, like flying pursuivant,
    Against foul fiends to aid us militant!
They for us fight, they watch and duly ward,
    And their bright squadrons round about us plant;
And all for love, and nothing for reward:
O! why should heavenly God to men have such regard?

EDMUND SPENSER

A cherub is a member of the second order of angels often represented as a winged child.

*R*ound us, too, shall angels shine,
such as ministered to thee.

GEORGE HUNT SMYTTEN

*W*e trust in plumed procession
For such the angels go—
Rank after Rank, with even feet—
And uniforms of Snow.

EMILY DICKINSON

For a good angel
will go with him,
his journey will
be successful,
and he will come home
safe and sound.

APOCRYPHA, TOBIAS 5:21

guardian angel
o'er his life presiding,
Doubling his pleasures,
and his cares dividing.

SAMUEL ROGERS

*I*t is in rugged crises,

in unweariable endurance,

and in aims which put

sympathy out of the question,

that the angel is shown.

RALPH WALDO EMERSON

It is wonderful that every angel, in whatever direction he turns his body and face, sees the Lord in front of him.

EMANUEL SWEDENBORG

The angels laughed.

God looked down from his seventh heaven and smiled.

The angels spread their wings and, together with Elijah, flew upward into the sky.

Isaac Bashevis Singer

The Angels' Whisper

A baby was sleeping;
Its mother was weeping;
For her husband was far on the wild raging sea;
And the tempest was swelling
Round the fisherman's dwelling;
And she cried, "Dermot, darling, oh come back to me!"

Her beads while she number'd,
The baby still slumber'd,
And smiled in her face as she bended her knee:
"Oh, blest be that warning,
My child, thy sleep adorning,
For I know that the angels are whispering with thee!

"And while they are keeping
Bright watch o'er they sleeping,
Oh, pray to them softly, my baby, with me!
And say thou wouldst rather
They'd watch o'er thy father!
For I know that the angels are whispering to thee."

The dawn of the morning
Saw Dermot returning,
And the wife wept with joy her babe's father to see;
And closely caressing
Her child with a blessing,
Said, "I knew that the angels were whispering with thee."

Samuel Lover

For He shall give His angels charge over thee, to keep thee in all thy ways.

They shall bear thee up in their hands, lest thou dash thy foot against a stone.

PSALM 91:11-12

Better than beauty and than youth
Are saints and angels, a glad company.

DANTE GABRIEL ROSSETTI

*O*utside the open window

The morning air is all awash with angels.

RICHARD WILBUR

An angel can illumine the thought and mind of man by strengthening the power of vision, and by bringing within his reach some truth which the angel himself contemplates.

THOMAS AQUINAS

t is unnecessary to question me," he
said, "I understand what you think. You should
know that these beings are men like you were
once, before God began to create you. Ask this old
man one day to lead you into Infinity. Then you
will see what God plans to do with you and you
will learn that today you are far from completion.
What would the work of the Creator be if it were
all done in a day? God never rests."

The old man vanished and I awoke, lifting my
gaze heavenward to see the white-winged angel
soaring toward the stars, his long, fair hair leaving
a trail of light in the firmament.

PAUL GAUGUIN

Angels, in the early morning
May be seen the Dews among,
Stooping—plucking—smiling—flying—
Do the Buds to them belong?
Angels, when the sun is hottest
May be seen the sands among,
Stooping—plucking—sighing—flying—
Parched the flowers they bear along.

EMILY DICKINSON

Sometimes on lonely mountain-meres
    I find a magic bark;
I leap on board: no helmsman steers:
    I float till all is dark.
A gentle sound, an awful light!
    Three angels bear the holy Grail:
With folded feet, in stoles of white,
    On sleeping wings they sail.
Ah, blessed vision! blood of God!
    My spirit beats her mortal bars,
As down dark tides the glory slides,
    And star-like mingles with the stars.

ALFRED, LORD TENNYSON

Jacob dreamed,
and behold
a ladder set up
on the earth,
and the top
of it reached
to Heaven;
and behold
the angels of
God ascending
and descending
on it.

GENESIS 28:12

And yet, as angels in some brighter
dreams
Call to the soul when man doth
sleep,
So some strange thoughts transcend
our wonted themes,
And into glory peep.

HENRY VAUGHAN

None sing so wildly well
As the angel Israfel
And the giddy stars
   (so legends tell)
Ceasing their hymns,
   attend the spell
Of his voice, all mute.

EDGAR ALLAN POE

Angels from friendship

gather half their joy.

EDWARD YOUNG

*A*round our pillows golden ladders rise,

And up and down the skies,

With winged sandals shod,

The angels come, and go, the Messengers of God!

Nor, though they fade from us, do they depart—

R. H. Stoddard

The angel Gabriel was sent from God unto a city of Galilee, named Nazareth.

To a virgin espoused to a man whose name was Joseph, of the house of David; and the virgin's name was Mary.

And the angel came in unto her, and said, Hail, thou that art highly favored, the Lord is with thee: blessed art thou among women.

LUKE 1:26-28

There were . . . shepherds abiding in the field, keeping watch over their flock by night.

And, lo, the angel of the Lord came upon them, and the glory of the Lord shone round about them, and they were sore afraid.

And the angel said unto them, "Fear not, for behold, I bring you good tidings of great joy, which shall be to all people.

For unto you is born this day in the city of David, a savior, which is Christ the Lord."

LUKE 2:8-11

Hark! the herald angels sing
Glory to the newborn King.
Peace on earth, and mercy mild,
God and sinners reconciled.
Joyful all ye nations, rise,
Join the triumph of the skies;
With the Angelic host proclaim,
"Christ is born in Bethlehem,"
Hark! the herald angels sing·
Glory to the newborn King.

CHARLES WESLEY

NOW·LETTEST·THOV·THY·
SERVANT·DEPART·IN·PEACE.

PEACE·
ON·EARTH·

GOOD·WILL·
TOWARD·MEN·

Angels and archangels may have
    gathered there,
Cherubim and seraphim thronged
    the air;
But his mother only, in her maiden
    bliss,
Worshipped the beloved with a kiss.

CHRISTINA ROSSETTI

To love for the sake of

being loved is human,

but to love for the

sake of loving is angelic.

ALPHONSE DE LAMARTINE

Twice or thrice had I loved thee,
Before I knew thy face or name.
So in a voice, so in a shapeless flame,
Angels affect us oft, and worshipped be.

JOHN DONNE

Abou Ben Adhem and the Angel

Abou Ben Adhem—may his tribe increase—
Awoke one night from a deep dream of peace,
And saw within the moonlight in his room,
Making it rich and like a lily in bloom,
An angel writing in a book of gold.
Exceeding peace had made Ben Adhem bold,
And to the presence in the room he said:
"What writest thou?" The vision raised its head,
And with a look made all of sweet accord,
Answered: "The names of those who love the Lord."
"And is mine one?" said Abou. "Nay, not so,"
Replied the angel. Abou spoke more low,
But cheerly still; and said: "I pray thee, then,
Write me as one that loves his fellowmen."
The angel wrote, and vanished. The next night
It came again with a great wakening light,
And shewed the names whom love of God had blessed,
And lo! Ben Adhem's name led all the rest.

LEIGH HUNT

Angels descending,
  bringing from above,
Echoes of mercy, whispers of love.

FANNY J. CROSBY

*T*hen too when angel voices sung

The mercy of their God, and strung

Their harps to hail, with welcome sweet,

That moment watched for by all eyes.

THOMAS MOORE

*U*nless you can love, as the angels may,
With the breadth of heaven betwixt you;
Unless you can dream that his faith is fast,
Through behoving and unbehoving;
Unless you can die when the dream is past—
Oh, never call it loving!

ROBERT BROWNING

*usic is well said
to be the speech of angels.*

Thomas Carlyle

If I have freedom in my love,

And in my soul am free,

Angels alone that soar above

Enjoy such liberty.

RICHARD LOVELACE

Ring out ye crystal spheres,
Once bless our human ears
(If ye have power to touch our senses so)
And let your silver chime
Move in melodious time;
And let the base of heav'ns' deep organ blow,
And with your ninefold harmony
Make up full consort to th' angelic symphony.

JOHN MILTON

The Guardian Angel

Dear and great Angel, wouldst thou only leave
That child, when thou hast done with him, for me!
Let me sit all the day here, that when eve
    Shall find performed thy special ministry
And time come for departure, thou, suspending
Thy flight, mayst see another child for tending,
    Another still, to quiet and retrieve.

Then I shall feel thee step one step, no more,
From when thou standest now, to where I gaze,
—And suddenly my head is covered o'er
    With those wings, white above the child who prays
Now on that tomb—and I shall feel thee guarding
Me, out of all the world; for me, discarding
    Yon Heaven thy home, that waits and opes its door!

ROBERT BROWNING

I have no angels left
	Now, Sweet, to pray to:
Where you have made your shrine
	They are away to.
They have struck Heaven's tent,
	And gone to cover you:
Whereso you keep your state
	Heaven is pitched over you.

FRANCIS THOMPSON

*A*nd with the morn, those angel faces smile

Which I have loved long since, and lost awhile.

John Henry, Cardinal Newman

Ministering Angels

Angels of light, spread your bright wings and keep
    Near me at morn:
Nor in the starry eve, nor midnight deep,
    Leave me forlorn.

From all dark spirits of unholy power
    Guard my weak heart,
Circle around me in each perilous hour,
    And take my part.

From all foreboding thoughts and dangerous fears,
    Keep me secure;
Teach me to hope, and through the bitterest tears
    Still to endure.

If lonely in the road so fair and wide
    My feet should stray,
Then through a rougher, safer pathway guide
    Me day by day.

Should my heart faint at its unequal strife,
    O still be near!
Shadow the perilous sweetness of this life
    With holy fear.

Then leave me not alone in this bleak world,
    Where'er I roam,
And at the end, with your bright wings unfurled,
    O take me home!

ADELAIDE A. PROCTER

The Two Angels

Two angels, one of Life and one of Death,
    Passed o'er our village as the morning broke;
The dawn was on their faces, and beneath,
    The somber houses hearsed with plumes of smoke.

Their attitude and aspect were the same,
    Alike their features and their robes of white;
But one was crowned with amaranth, as with flame,
    And one with asphodels, like flakes of light.

I saw them pause on their celestial way;
    Then said I, with deep fear and doubt oppressed,
"Beat not so loud, my heart, lest thou betray
    The place where thy beloved are at rest!"

HENRY WADSWORTH LONGFELLOW

Matthew, Mark, Luke, and John
Bless the bed that I lie on.
Four corners to my bed,
Four angels there be spread:
One at the head, one at the feet,
And two to guard me while I sleep.

Listening Angels

Blue against the bluer heavens
   Stood the mountain, calm and still,
Two white Angels, bending earthward,
   Leant upon the hill.

Listening leant those silent Angels,
   And I also longed to hear
What sweet strain of earthly music
   Thus could charm their ear.

I heard the sound of many trumpets
   In a warlike march draw nigh;
Solemnly a mighty army
   Passed in order by.

But the clang had ceased; the echoes
   Soon had faded from the hill;
While the Angels, calm and earnest
   Leant and listened still.

Then I heard a fainter clamor,
   Forge and wheel were clashing near,
And the Reapers in the meadow
   Singing loud and clear.

When the sunset came in glory,
   And the toil of day was o'er,
Still the Angels leant in silence,
   Listening as before.

Then, as daylight slowly vanished,
   And the evening mists grew dim,
Solemnly from distant voices
   Rose a vesper hymn.

ADELAIDE A. PROCTER

In this dim world of clouding cares,
    We rarely know, till 'wildered eyes
    See white wings lessening up the skies,
The Angels with us unawares.

GERALD MASSEY

When the chant was done, and lingering
  Died upon the evening air,
From the hill the radiant Angels
  Still were listening there.

Silent came the gathering darkness,
  Bringing with it sleep and rest;
Save a little bird was singing
  Near her leafy nest.

Through the sounds of war and labor
   She had warbled all day long,
While the Angels leant and listened
   Only to her song.

But the starry night was coming;
   When she ceased her little lay,
From the mountaintop the Angels
   Slowly passed away.

             ADELAIDE A. PROCTER

In the Heavenly Meadow

To Heaven's Meadows, bright with flowers and sunshine,
    The little children go,
When they have had enough of life's sad dreaming,
    And leave the earth below.

But as they had not time to learn their lessons
    Before they went away,
There is a school, where all the angel children
    Must work four hours a day.

With golden pencils upon silver tablets,
    They copy fairy tales,
And learn to keep their halos bright and shining,
    And sing, and play their scales.

And twice a week they glide with merry laughter
    All down the Milky Way,
And homeward in the evening wander softly
    Upon a sunset ray.

But Sunday is the day they love and long for;
    Then all the children go
And play from morn till night within a meadow
    Where flowers in thousands grow.

The meadow is not green, but blue and golden,
    The flowers like dewdrops bright;
When it is night, they burn and glow and glisten—
    Men call them stars of light.

KATE E. BUNCE

The Angel

"Whenever a child dies, an angel comes down from heaven, takes the child in its arms, and, spreading out its large white wings, visits all the places that had been particularly dear to the child. From the best-loved place the angel gathers a handful of flowers, flying up again to heaven with them. There they bloom more beautifully than on earth. But that flower which is most loved receives a voice, so that it can join the song of the chorus of bliss."

Thus spoke an angel while carrying a child up to heaven. And the child listened as in a dream. And they visited the places that had been most dear to the child, and where the little one had often played, passing through gardens full of the most beautiful flowers.

"Which flowers shall we take with us to plant in heaven?" the angel asked.

Now there stood a solitary rosebush of extraordinary beauty, but a mischievous hand had wantonly broken the stem, so that all the branches, recently of such a beautiful green, laden with half-opened buds, hung down, withered and sad, upon the mossy ground below.

"Oh, that dear little bush!" the child sighed. "Let us take it with us so that in heaven it may again bloom."

The angel took the rosebush, kissing the child at the same time, and the little thing half opened its eyes. The angel gathered some lovely flowers, the perfume and colors of which were delightful, as well as a few humble buttercups and wild pansies.

"Now we have flowers," the child said, and the angel nodded. But still they did not fly up to heaven.

It was night, and all was quiet; but they remained in the large town, hovering over one of the narrowest streets, where there were heaps of straw, ashes, and all manner of rubbish, for it was a day when many people change their lodgings. There lay broken plates, pieces of plaster, the crowns of old hats, and rags of all kinds—in short, a mass of things in no way pleasing to the eye.

The angel pointed down among all this rubbish to some pieces of a broken flowerpot, and a lump of earth which had fallen out of it, held together by the roots of a withered wildflower, which had been thrown among the rubbish.

"That we will take with us," the angel said. "I will tell you why as we fly on."

And the angel spoke thus:—

"There below, in that narrow lane, in a cellar, lived a poor, sick boy, who from his earliest years had been bedridden. Even on his best days he could only manage to walk around the little room a couple of times on his crutches. On some days during the summer, the sun's rays shone upon the floor of the cellar for half an hour. When the boy sat there warming himself in the sun, and wondering at the red blood which he saw through his thin fingers as he held them up to his face, he would say, 'Today I have been out.' He only knew of the green forest when the son of a neighbor brought him the first branch of a beech tree that was out in leaf. He held it over his head, imagining that he was in the forest under the beech trees, with the sun shining and birds singing.

"One day in spring the neighbor's son brought him some wildflowers, among which there happened to be one that had its roots, and it was set in a pot and placed near his bed. The flower flourished, sending forth new shoots. It blossomed every year, so that it became the sick boy's flower garden, his greatest comfort and treasure on earth. He watered it and watched it, and took care that it had the benefit of even the last ray of the sun which glided through the low window. The flower entwined itself in his dreams, for it blossomed for him alone, delighting him with its scent and its beautiful colors. It gladdened his eyes, and to the flower he turned, even in death. It is now a year he has been in heaven, and for a year the flower has stood, forgotten and dried-up in the window, until today during the moving, it was thrown out into the street. And that is the flower, the poor withered flower, which we have added to our bouquet, for it has given more pleasure than the most beautiful flower in the garden of a queen."

"And how do you know all this?" the child asked.

"I know it," the angel answered, "because I myself was that poor sick boy who walked on crutches. I know my flower well."

Then the child opened its eyes, and looked up into the angel's beautiful face, which beamed with happiness, and at the same moment they were in heaven, where joy and bliss reigned. The child received wings like the other angel, and they flew about together, hand in hand. The flowers received renewed life; but the poor withered wildflower received a voice and sang with the angels, with whom the whole space of the heavens was filled, in circles, one row behind the other, further and further back, and so on to infinity, all being equally happy.

All sang praises and thanksgivings—the child just received into heaven, and the poor wildflower which had been cast away on a heap of rubbish in a narrow, dark street.

HANS CHRISTIAN ANDERSEN

LOVE AND DEATH

What time the mighty moon was gathering light
Love paced the thymy plots of Paradise,
And all about him roll'd his lustrous eyes;
When, turning round a cassia, full in view,
Death, walking all alone beneath a yew,
And talking to himself, first met his sight:
"You must begone," said Death, "these walks are mine,"
Love wept and spread his sheeny vans for flight;
Yet ere he parted said, "This hour is thine:
Thou art the shadow of life, and as the tree
Stands in the sun and shadows all beneath,
So in the light of great eternity
Life eminent creates the shade of death;
The shadow passeth when the tree shall fall,
But I shall reign for ever over all."

ALFRED, LORD TENNYSON

*G*ood-night, sweet prince,
And flights of angels sing thee to thy rest!

WILLIAM SHAKESPEARE